MINNESOTA TWINS

BOB HINZ

CREATIVE EDUCATION

Strong lightweight. Darrell Jackson erased the powerful Royals in the 1980 contest.

ISBN 0-87191-865-X

MINNESOTA TWINS

THINK, HUSTLE, WIN. The HUSTLE sign got a big dent in '64, from a bat swung in frustration. But no signs were hit during the '65 campaign. The Twins were having their finest year ever.

HOW MINNESOTA GOT ITS BASEBALL TEAM

Minnesota is the "Land of 10,000 Lakes." Beautiful lakes, teeming with fish just begging to be caught.

In the spring of 1961, however, few Minnesotans were baiting their hooks. From Minnehaha to Bigfork, the people of Minnesota had caught something new—baseball fever!

Calvin Griffith, the owner of the Washington Senators baseball team, got things started. When the fans in Washington D.C. stopped supporting the Senators, Griffith moved the team to the "Twin Cities" of Minneapolis-St. Paul. There, the Senators were renamed the Minnesota Twins.

Minnesotans couldn't have been happier. On Opening Day—April 26, 1961—24,000 excited fans hustled into Metropolitan Stadium to welcome their new team. Griffith was happy, too. It was a welcome change from those tiny crowds in Washington D.C.

In the Twins' first year, nearly 1,500,000 fans came to cheer. Others listened faithfully on their radios.

Hot cornerman. John Castino anchors the Twins with a quick toss to first for the out.

Twins

The enthusiasm of the fans paid off. It sparked the Twins to a pennant in only five years. If that wasn't enough excitement, the World Series was just around the corner. But, of course, that's getting ahead of the story. First . . .

A PENNANT FOR THE PEOPLE

The year was 1965. If you lived in Minnesota, the terrible weather ran your life. You woke to the task of shoveling huge drifts of snow from the driveway. You pumped rainwater out of your flooded basement. Or, you sprinted around the neighborhood, chasing down roof shingles in the gales.

Though the weather was cold, the Minnesota Twins were hot. From the first few games of the 1965 season, it was obvious that the Twins had the American League Pennant on their minds. If the fans were surprised, enemy teams were astonished. After all, this was the same team that had finished sixth a year earlier, 20 games behind the front-runners. But Manager Sam Mele had used spring training to teach his team a daring new style of play.

In 1965, the Twins were battling for the American League pennant when Sam Mele patiently sat through this rain-out.

SAM FOR PRESIDENT
As the Twins gained momentum in the '60s, the red-white-and-blue buttons began showing up on loyal fans: "Sam Mele for President" and "Harmon Killebrew for Governor."

NUMBER RETIRED
No. 3 was never worn across a broader set of shoulders than those of Harmon Killebrew. In honor of this great Twins ballplayer, the Minnesota club officially retired No. 3 in 1975.

Now, "hit-and-run" had become the Twins' way of life. They stole lots of bases. They stretched singles into doubles and triples. They shook the confidence of their opponents, and squeezed out the winning run.

"What they did," said Birdie Tebbets of the Cleveland Indians, "was to take a run at everybody and just beat 'em back."

The 1965 Twins demolished the mighty Yankees by taking 13 out of 18 games. They weren't much easier on the White Sox (11 of 18). And they showed no mercy in their games with the Senators and Red Sox (32 of 36).

They dared to be different, to be swifter, bolder, more daring, and more confident.

When asked why he pitched so fast, league leader Jim Grant said: "With the kind of stuff I've got, it isn't worth thinking about what you're doing. Just grab the ball and let it go."

After swatting a game-winning homer against the White Sox, Jimmie Hall said: "I don't truly know what kind of pitch the man threw me. I just swing the bat and hope for the best."

Mudcat wings one in. Jim "Mudcat" Grant gave the Dodgers a pitching lesson in this 1965 win for the Twins.

Twins
32

32

Future MVP Zoilo Versalles put it this way: "If you get to one base and you can see the ball on the ground in the outfield, run like crazy to the next base."

Here was a ballclub that *deserved* to win the Pennant. Now, for only the second time in the last 20 years, a World Series would open in an American League stadium not built by Babe Ruth. The stadium was named Metropolitan, smack dab in the middle of the twin cities.

THE WORLD SERIES

No one really expected the L.A. Dodgers to roll over and play dead, but the Twins did take the first two games with surprising ease, whipping Dodger aces Don Drysdale and Sandy Koufax, 8-2 and 5-1.

Then the next three games were played in Los Angeles, where the home-field advantage continued. There, the Dodger pitchers roared back. Claude Osteen took Game #3 with a 4-0 shutout; Drysdale took Game #4, 7-2. And Koufax tossed a 7-0 shutout in Game #5.

Minnesota got the final two games on home turf, and

Vic Power beats the ball and scores against the legendary Elston Howard of the Yankees. (1962).

ROOKIE PITCHING RECORD
The most games ever pitched in a rookie season came from Doug Corbett, who hurled 73 for Minnesota in '80.

FANS LOVE MARTIN
Loud and colorful, Manager Billy Martin was not too popular with the Twins' players, but he did get the club to the '69 A.L. West title. After losing in the playoffs, Martin was given the boot by owners, much to the displeasure of the fans, who loved the fiery manager.

they took quick advantage in Game #6 with a 5-1 win, pitched by Mudcat Grant.

The showdown game featured Jim Kaat against Koufax. Through three innings, it remained a no-score contest. Then Dodger Lou Johnson drew first blood, sending a home-run souvenir into the stands. Before the 4th was over, the Dodgers had punched another run, and led 2-0.

Koufax, meanwhile, was hurting on the mound. With only two days rest, his left elbow ached with each pitch. Unable to control his curve, Sandy stuck with his fastball which was still plenty baffling for the Twins' sluggers.

The Twins had runners on first and second in the fifth, when Zoilo Versalles slammed a sure double down the third-base line. But wait! Junior Gilliam leaped toward the ball and made a stabbing catch for out number three. Oomph!

The Twins were crushed. Koufax went on to pitch a 2-0 shutout, handing the Dodgers their third World Championship in a row.

Sure, the Twins were disappointed, but they could still hold their heads high. They had pushed the series to the

Former Yankee star Billy Martin (center) came to the Twins to coach in the '60s.

Twins
Twins

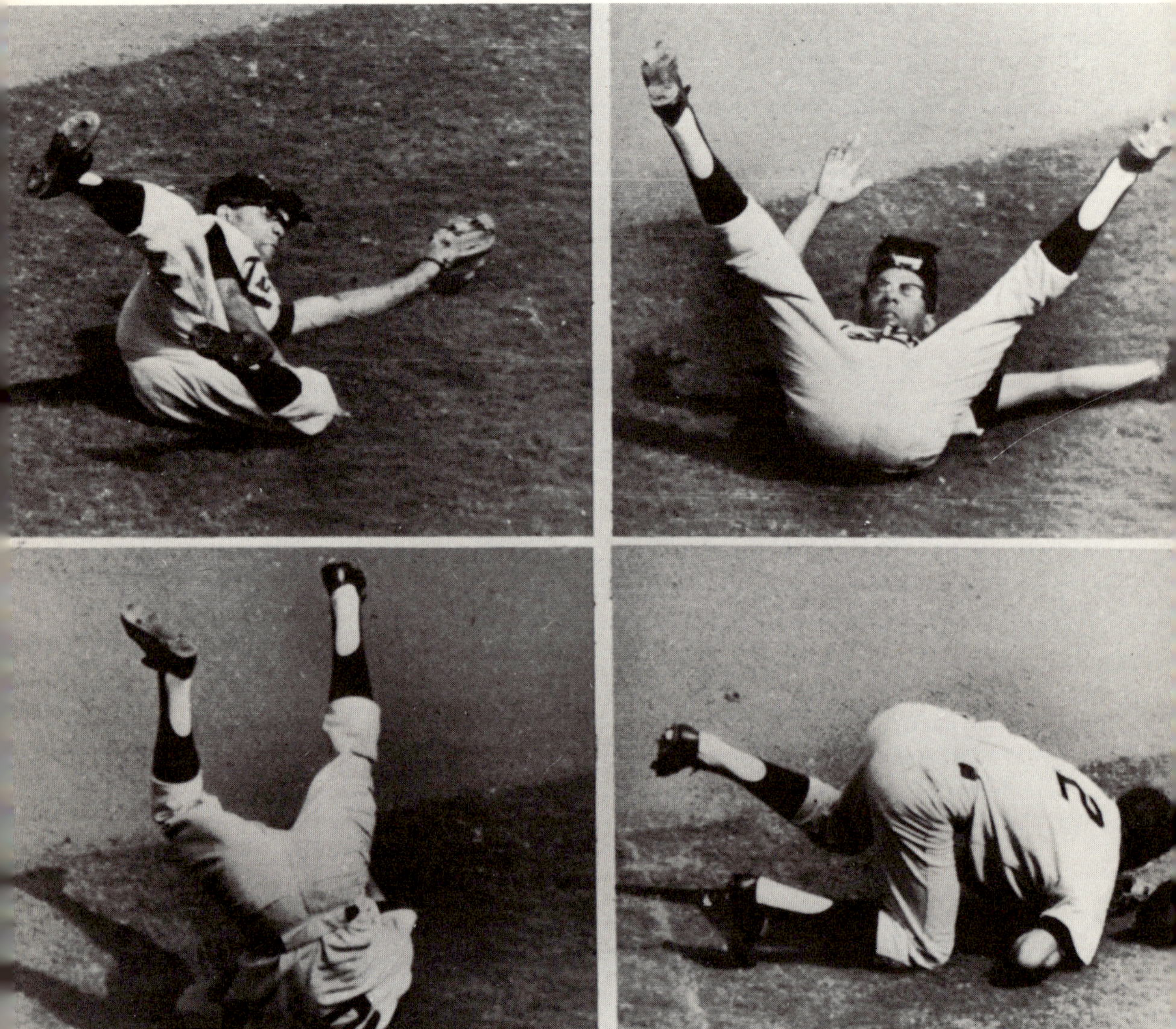

maximum—seven games against one of the finest Dodger teams in the history of baseball. The Twins had earned a reputation in that Series, and they let it be known that they'd be back.

VERSALLES SPARKS THE TEAM

No one athlete is totally responsible for a team's success. Sometimes, though, there's one certain guy who inspires others and leads the way. In the mid-1960s, the spark plug for the Twins was Zoilo Versalles.

At 5′10″, 155-pounds, Zoilo was the Club leader in stolen bases and a powerful lead-off hitter. There's no question that it was Zoilo who led the Twins to the World Series, and kept them pumped up after the disappointing loss to L.A.

Zoilo Versalles was as fast on his feet as he was with a bat. He led the American League in runs scored in '65, was second in hits, first in doubles, second in triples, third in stolen bases. And first in the hearts of Twins' fans. Oh yes, and he was also the American League's MVP.

Zoilo the acrobat. Zoilo Versalles makes a rolling, tumbling try for a shot off the bat of Dodger Ron Fairly.

KOOSMAN STRIKES
Jerry Koosman came to the mound loose as a goose on June 23, 1980 against Kansas City. By game's end, he had collected 15 strikeouts, the best A.L. effort that year.

***RECORD SEASON** Minnesota's all-time season attendance mark was set in 1967 when 1,438,547 fans came to see the Twins in action. They were runner-up in that year's pennant race.*

It wasn't always this way for Versalles. When he came to the majors at age 18, he had some rough edges. Coach Ellis Clary of the Senators remembered: "I worked like a dog with the boy to teach him to play. He had all the tools but so many bad habits that it was like trying to get an alligator to play the piano."

Zoilo seemed cocky, but actually he was just afraid to fail. "I got to the ballpark at 6 a.m.," he said. "I looked at the stadium and then went five miles away and sat in a park and listened to the birds wake up. Inside me, I knew I was not going to make it."

Senators Manager Cookie Lavagetto recalled that Versalles would run into the clubhouse and hide if he made an error.

Still, Versalles moved confidently into the '65 season at the top of his form, thanks in part to coach Billy Martin's grooming. Martin had a calming effect, bringing Zoilo's talent into play.

"In other years," said Zoilo before the '65 Series, "I played hard, but it wasn't fun. This time it was fun

Harry (Cookie) Lavagetto, left, shows off a new name in the league to Yankee manager Ralph Houk. (1961).

Minnesota
TWINS

because Billy Martin helped make me the complete ballplayer.

"This thrill of playing in the World Series is so deep inside me that only I know what it is."

Coach Billy Martin smiled and nodded. Versalles, the kid, had become Versalles, the confident pro.

HARMON KILLEBREW COMES TO TOWN

After the '65 Series, the Twins settled down to a contender role in '66 and '67, finishing in the runner-up position, playing .549 and .562 ball. Then in '68 they slipped to .488 before rebounding to a fine .599 season in '69. That effort earned them the American League West title, as they rolled to a 97-65 mark.

These building years were also growing years for an outstanding baseball player named Harmon Killebrew, one of the Twins' true treasures.

Harmon Killebrew was a 17-year-old kid when he began his career in major-league baseball in 1954. In a few short years, the sturdy, muscular young man established himself as the second most consistent hitter in

Harmon Killebrew, the fifth all-time home run hitter, just heard the news that he would be leaving the Twins for the Royals. (1974)

THE KILLEBREW RECORD BOOK

Harmon Killebrew has more records than any other player in Twins' history: Most full seasons (14); most games (1,939); most at-bats (6,593); most runs (1,047); most total bases (3,412); most home runs (475); most RBI (1,325); most bases-on-balls (1,321); and most strike outs (1,314).

BATBOY TO PRESIDENT
Calvin R. Griffith, president and chairman of the board of the Minnesota Twins, got his start in baseball when he worked as a batboy for the 1922 Washington Senators, a team he'd later move to the twin cities of Minneapolis-St. Paul.

baseball history—runner-up only to Babe Herman Ruth. As his career with the Twins stretched into the '70s, Killebrew's stats showed an average of one home run every 12.9 times at the bat—just a notch behind Ruth's record of 11.8.

As he reached age 34, Harmon's hairline fell off to graying side fenders. His bottom grew heavy, and his midsection thickened. His right knee ached from an old injury, and he looked better-suited to be watching the game from a comfortable overstuffed chair in his living room.

But in truth, Harmon Killebrew was respected as one of the most dangerous all-around hitters in the American League. In 1970, he led the majors in home runs and RBI, and was named the A.L.'s Most Valuable Player.

One year later he was surging toward his first 50-home-run season, batting well over .300.

A proud man, Killebrew had a no-nonsense attitude in the batter's box. Waiting his turn in the on-deck circle, he'd slip on his hard hat, standing absolutely still at the bat rack, glaring at the pitcher.

The incredible Dean Chance (left) matched up well against Luis Tiant of Cleveland (right), but a trade was just around the corner. (1969)

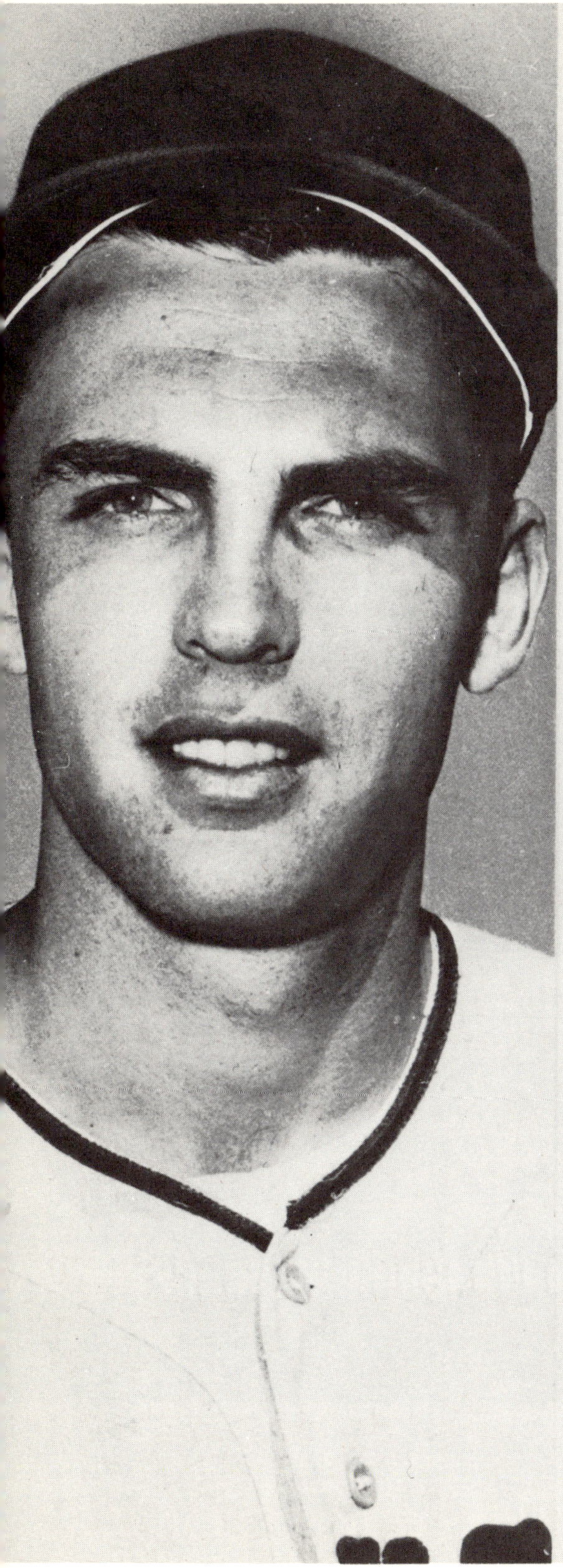

When he took the on-deck spot, Harmon exercised three, maybe four ferocious swings to remind himself of the task at hand; then he'd kneel and stare at the pitcher again.

Once in the batter's box, it was one calming swish of the lumber between pitches. Otherwise he stood absolutely still, with the bat just resting on his shoulder. "I'm not a fidgety person," he explained. "I try to stay as calm and relaxed as I can. It helps me concentrate, which I think is the most important thing about hitting."

If you observed the loud chatter and backslapping in the clubhouse after a Twins' victory, you'd seldom find Harmon involved. He even slipped away from the post-season celebration when the Twins won the A.L. West pennant in 1970.

Still, Harmon Killebrew was friendly and well-liked. Once, a stocky minor-leaguer arrived with sore legs, and Killebrew was among the first to stop and chat—Harmon had leg problems, too. He was happy to help if he could.

Baseball was a learning process for Killebrew. As the years rolled on, he learned to let bad pitches pass him

Fleet-footed Tony Oliva of the Twins steals another base in 1966 action against the Red Sox.

HOME-RUN KINGS
Leading the Twins in career home runs are Harmon Killebrew with 475, Tony Oliva with 220 and Bob Allison with 211.

THOSE SPEEDY TWINS
The Twins play a fast nine innings of baseball. Two hours, 29 minutes, to be exact. That's well under the 2:36 average in the American League, second only to speedy Seattle, who sprint along at a 2:25 average.

by. He walked more, improving his average. Of course, it certainly helped to have guys like Tony Oliva and Cesar Tovar—high-average hitters—in the line-up with him.

"Naturally I hope I've gotten smarter as I've gotten more experience," said Harmon, "but I can't get all that excited about the .300 thing. The important thing for me is to drive in runs and score them."

When an athlete built like Harmon Killebrew unleashes his "hardest swing," there's little doubt of the result. And if, toward the end of his magnificent career, his awkward gimping trot around the bases wasn't as fluid and youthful as a Mays or Aaron, it was still a beautiful part of baseball history, and certainly one of it's most powerful images, in the shadows of Ruth.

A TEEN-AGE STARTER BAFFLES THE PROS

1970 was a big year for Minnesota, as the Twins captured their second consecutive A.L. West title. Their 98-64 record earned them a very respectable .605.

Part of that season's success story was written by a teen-ager named Bert Blyleven.

Clever pitcher. Cesar Tovar could beat you with a wild array of pitches. (1968)

What's it like being a teen-age starter in the majors?

That thrill came to Bert Blyleven in 1970 when he got a call from the Minnesota Twins. He'd barely had time to remove his mortarboard and robe after graduating from Garden Grove High School in California.

A native of Zeist, Holland, Bert had come to the States at age six. He brought along a shy grin, bright clear eyes, and a heart as big as all outdoors.

"I first started thinking about coming to the majors when I was 8-0 in the Florida Instructional League," he said. "I wondered if I'd be ready, but now that I've been with the Twins and pitched, I'm not worried about it anymore."

Just 18 months before taking his first major-league starting assignment, Bert learned how to throw a curve from his high school catcher. That curve would cause problems for Bert, as well as the batters he faced.

"Everyone kept telling me I had a good curve. So when I got here I figured that's what I should throw. I was throwing it about 50-percent of the time, and after my sixth start or so, my elbow began bothering me.

Corkscrew. Bert Blyleven shut out the Milwaukee Brewers in this 1972 battle.

RED-HOT ROOKIES
Three Minnesota Twins began their major-league careers by winning the League's "Rookie-of-the-Year" award. They were Tony Oliva in '64, Rod Carew in '67, and Bert Blyleven in '70.

ALL-STAR LANDREAUX
The only Twin to make the 1980 All-Star roster was outfielder Ken Landreaux. It was Ken's first All-Star appearance, but it was the 14th appearance for former Twin Rod Carew, who was now playing for the California Angels.

"The doctor told me my arm was still growing and the curve hurt it. From then on, I only used it about 30-percent of the time," he said.

That was enough. Bert had come up with a frustrating mix for the opponents. With his new philosophy at work, he tossed a four-hitter against a fine Detroit Tiger ballclub, winning going away, 2-1. That victory moved him to a 4-3 record for the season, lowering his ERA to 2.58—best for Twins' starters.

While the mound was a source of real pleasure for young Blyleven, the off-hours proved long and lonesome. Living by himself that freshman year, he rarely saw his teammates after the final out of a game.

"They all go home to their families at night, and I can't get into the places where the other single guys go because I'm not old enough," he explained.

Though he was lonely that first year, Bert ended the season in fine fashion by walking off with the League's MVP honors for "Rookie of the Year."

Outfielder Larry Hisle shows the intensity that marked his play in 1974.

Twins

Twins

FROM PITCHER TO HITTER, DARWIN'S SWITCH WAS COMPLETE

The headline in the sports page read: "Darwin goes ape."

After Blyleven's amazing rookie season, the Twins stumbled the following year, dipping below .500 with a 74-86 record. But they got right up again in '72, to begin a comeback, finishing third in the A.L. West race, 81-81.

A portion of that turnaround came from the bat of Bobby Darwin.

The excitement was about Bobby Darwin, the Twins' 29-year-old rookie center-fielder whose bat was giving the ballclub a leaping start in the American League West. Quite a change from their fifth place finish the year before.

In fact, the entire '72 Twins' roster overflowed with new faces, 12 of them, to be exact. But it was Darwin's face and muscles that caught everyone's imagination whenever he stepped to the plate. The season began with games in four different ballparks. Darwin got a homer in each!

Easygoing Bob Darwin anchored the outfield in '74.

DON'T DIE IN JULY

There was no doubt the 1965 team was going all the way. As one fan reminded the doubtful: "This team does the impossible all the time. Why, this year they didn't even die in July. And the Twins always die in July."

31 RUNS IN ONE GAME! It was a day for the offense, when the Twins took on the Oakland A's on Apr. 27, 1980. When the dust settled, the Twins had 20 of the 31 runs scored in that game.

In Oakland, Darwin slapped the ball all the way into the upper deck—460 feet away. In Yankee Stadium, he selected a Mel Stottlemyre breaking ball and air-mailed it to an eager fan, 450 feet away.

"He's an amazing athlete," said Bob Rodgers, Minnesota's bullpen coach. "Everything stops when he comes up. Pitchers warming up will stop and stare until Bobby's through hitting. Nobody wants to miss his performance."

It's almost as if Darwin had planned an imitation of teammate Harmon Killebrew. Their homers could shadow one another on the slow-motion replay—rising high in the air and hanging for a moment before falling into the distant bleachers.

Bobby Darwin got his start as a pitcher. He was called up from San Jose by the Dodgers at age 19. His debut was terrible. It lasted three innings, got him an ERA of 12.0 and a ticket back to the minors. He stayed on the mound, but his 42-50 stats through 1970 weren't getting him up the ladder. So he made the change to hitter, and found his average moving upward—.297 in a winter league, then soaring to .488 in exhibition play.

Heading into the 1970s, Twins coach Bob Rodgers had a plan.

TC
Twins
10

With the Dodger roster checkered with big-name outfielders like Willie Davis, Willie Crawford, Manny Mota, Richie Allen and Bill Russell, there simply wasn't room for a Bobby Darwin. But Minnesota had room, and the trade was made.

The Twins issued him No. 53 during the Florida training session. The kids would occasionally beckon him, shouting: "Hey, 53, how 'bout signing an autograph?"

When the team returned to league play, Bobby sported a No. 2 on his back. The kids still shouted for his autograph, but with a slightly different tone: "Mr. Darwin, please." It was a tribute to the man, and his struggle for a bit of the limelight, a touch of fame. Bobby Darwin had arrived as a professional, and the kids paid him the proper respect.

But the press had seen stars come and go, glimmer and dim over the years. Still, they gathered round the powerful Darwin, asking the ordinary questions—"Are you for real?", "How did you change?", "Why did you change?"

Bobby soothed himself during those interviews by

The great Lyman Bostock pauses for a moment at 1975 Spring training in Tampa.

DIPLOMAT
Growing up as a youth, Rod Carew spent lots of time swimming in the Panama Canal. Later he attended the same New York high school as U.S. diplomat Henry Kissinger.

NEW FENCES TO CLEAR ***Kicking off the '82 season, the Minnesota fans had a new ballpark to call home, and the Minnesota hitters had new fences to clear: 326 feet to rightfield, 406 feet to center, and 354 feet to left.***

constantly rubbing the barrel of his new bat with a bone. It was a tradition rarely seen since Ty Cobb had clobbered countless pitches with his bone-hardened bat many decades ago.

So what did Bobby Darwin enjoy most about his shining hour?

"Maybe the thing I like the best is seeing the ball go over some outfielder's head and into the stands. I enjoy seeing the pitcher drop his head in disgust. Remember, it used to be my head dropping, my pitches being hit out of ball parks.

The remainder of the '70s were laced with tough times for the Twins' ballclub. The best they could manage was third place, and their win-loss percentage hovered around .500. Not quite good enough against teams like New York and Baltimore, Kansas City and California. Still, there were plenty of enjoyable moments for the fans, especially during the "Carew years."

Mike Cubbage proved himself an eagle-eyed infielder in 1979.

Twins

2

ROD CAREW – A HITTING MACHINE

In 1975, Rod Carew joined a special circle of baseball giants when he became a member of the "four-straight big-league batting championships" club. The only other players to match this feat were Ty Cobb, Honus Wagner and Rogers Hornsby.

Carew got his "four-straight" with percentages of .318 ('72), .350 ('73), .364 ('74), and .359 ('75). Before that, he collected a single crown in '69 with a .332 average.

As a youth growing up in the Panama Canal, Rod had but one dream: Coming to America and playing big-league ball. That dream began to come true at age 15 when he came to Manhattan, N.Y. Although he spoke broken English and was "an outsider" to his classmates at George Washington High School, his performance on the baseball diamond quickly earned him lots of respect.

That respect was even greater during the '70s when Rod rewrote the book on hitting. Never one to back off, Carew took his "four-straight" batting championships and added two more—a total of seven crowns in the A.L. batter's box!

The one-and-only Rod Carew earned his batting crowns with a soft touch rather than power.

A CAREW CUT
Opponents grumble about Rod Carew's ability to slice the ball through holes in the defense. Says Rod: "I hit the ball to the opposite field so much that sometimes they'll move everybody to the left side against me."

A DENT IN HUSTLE
In the '60s, the Twins hung three signs in the walkway between the clubhouse and the dugout. The signs read: THINK, HUSTLE, WIN. The HUSTLE sign got a big dent in '64, from a bat swung in frustration. But no signs were hit during the '65 campaign. The Twins were having their finest year ever.

"He swings his bat about as perfectly as anyone I've seen," said Cleveland's Frank Robinson.

"He has an uncanny ability to move the ball around as if the bat were some kind of magic wand," said Oakland's Kenny Holtzman.

At one point during the '75 campaign, Rod was stroking the ball at a .418 clip. Talk was non-stop. Nobody had stayed over .400 since Ted Williams managed the impossible in '41. Carew didn't keep his numbers either. But he was still miles ahead of the competition.

"Carew watches the defense and hits according to how they play him," said Jim Northrup of the Orioles.

"It looks like he tries to take the ball and dunk it over the infielders' heads or hit it where they ain't," said Mickey Lolich of Detroit.

Carew denies any magic powers with the bat, but he does have a favorite hit: "One that's just one inch or two outside a guy's reach. Maybe he cheated over a step in the other direction on me, and I kept him honest."

While Ted Williams sported a "wait-for-the-right-pitch" philosophy, Carew disagrees. "My own theory is swing

Leo Cardenas gave the Twins new life in 1971.

TC
Twins
4

the bat. If the ball's around the plate, swing and make contact," he explains.

He doesn't even anticipate the pitcher's choice. "If I could be a guess hitter, I'd hit .500. But I don't like to think too much about hitting. I like being up there, not guessing, just getting up there and swinging free."

There are times when the bunt plays, too. Ask California's Ken McMullen about his frustration the day Carew bunted for two straight base hits against the swift third baseman. McMullen kept coming in closer, closer, until he could almost reach out and touch Carew. But Rod still layed down a third perfect bunt. McMullen still couldn't throw him out, but he did throw his glove, in frustration!

There would come a time when Rod Carew would leave the Minnesota Twins to finish out his career with the California Angels. But Minnesota fans would always hold a special place in their hearts for the man who provided bright moments during the most frustrating years for the Twins. Rod Carew — the only player in the modern era to win seven consecutive batting crowns.

Popular outfielder Steve Braun also served a term with the Seattle Mariners.

CAPTAIN HOOK Twins' Manager Bill Rigney earned the reputation of "Captain Hook" for the way he removed his starting pitchers off the mound.

THE GREAT WILFONG
For the '80 season, second baseman Rob Wilfong set an A.L. fielding record at his position when he snatched balls at a .9948 clip.

THE '80s: A NEW HOME, NEW DREAMS

The Twins opened the '82 season with new hopes and a new ballpark. Officially named the Hubert H. Humphrey Metrodome, the handsome weatherproof structure has a 10-acre roof made of teflon-coated fiberglass. Like a balloon, the roof is supported by air pressure maintained inside the Metrodome.

Twins' fans now have 54,500 armchair-style seats for their comfort, all nicely situated inside the climate-controlled arena.

Looking to recover from a cellar finish in '81, the Twins are rebuilding toward another championship. Gone are Killebrew, Oliva and Carew—men whose talent raised the Twins to championship calibre. But in their place have come guys like Doug Corbett, Ken Landreaux, Jerry Koosman, Peter Redfern, Roy Smalley, Rob Wilfong and Butch Wynegar. These men are determined to take their rightful places alongside the Minnesota superstars of the past. And you can rest assured that the loyal Minnesota fans will be there to watch it happen.

In 1979 Roy Smalley sparked his teammates through the long days of late August.

Twins

Rob Wilfong fell after snagging a Boston liner — but he hung onto the ball.